God is Speaking to You

JACQUI D. WILLIAMS

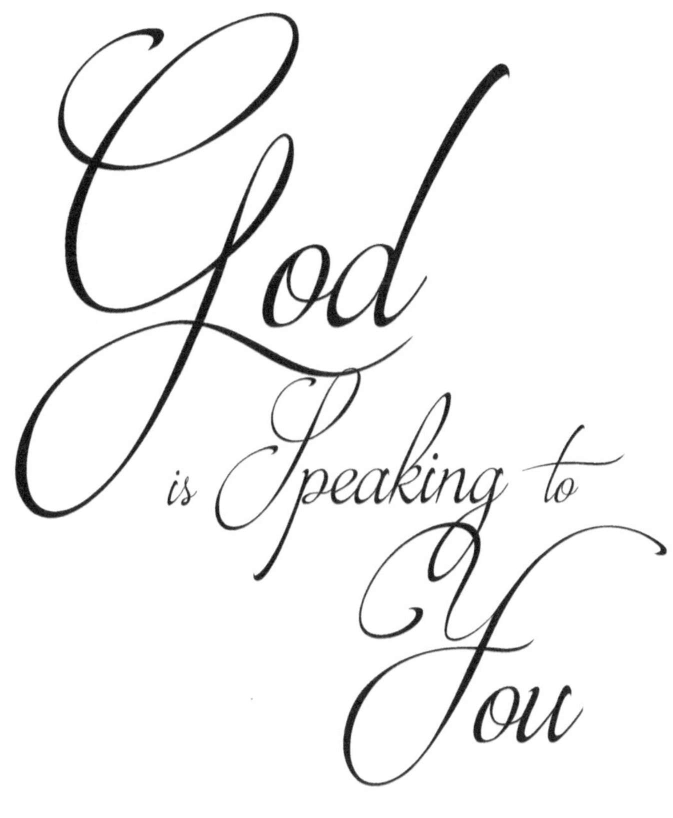

God is Speaking to You

JACQUI D. WILLIAMS

Christian Faith
PUBLISHING

ISBN 979-8-88616-344-5 (paperback)
ISBN 979-8-88616-345-2 (digital)

Christian Faith Publishing
832 Park Avenue
Meadville, PA 16335
www.christianfaithpublishing.com

All scriptures are taken from the Holy Bible, KJV

Printed in the United States of America

To God, the Almighty, and Awesome, I AM!

God Is

always ready and available to
meet you where you are.

Speaking

is something God does every time
you read His written Word.

To You

and for every person who reads this
book, my prayer is that as you spend
time in His Word, you will know when
it is God's voice speaking to you.

CONTENTS

Chapter 1
God's Written Word 1

Chapter 2
The Prophetic Message 9

Chapter 3
Knowing God's Voice 17

Chapter 4
God Speaks to the Backslider 23

Chapter 5
You Are Forgiven 30

Chapter 6
Be Constant in Prayer 35

Chapter 7
Honoring God: The Awesome I AM! 43

God's Written Word

Have you ever said, "How do I know when it is God speaking to me?" Let me tell you, God is speaking to you every day. When you spend time in God's Word, that is God speaking to you personally. I know you might be still saying, "Well, I have heard that before." I know God speaks to me through His written Word, but I need His direction for the personal areas of my life. I need specifics. I want to know that I have clarity in hearing God's voice before I take this job or before I decide to marry this person.

Unfortunately, you will not find personal specifics in the Bible where it tells you to marry a person or to take a particular job, but when you receive Jesus as Lord of your life, you have something even better. You have a relationship between you and God where you are now getting to know Him in a close and personal way. You are gaining and understanding more of what He wants for your personal life. Through God's Word, you learn His heart and His ways, and you will see God speaking to your personal situations through and by His Holy Spirit.

Before we look for God to speak to us, we must first begin by building a relationship by speaking to Him. I would find it somewhat presumptuous on our part to expect a miraculous direction for our situations when we have never taken the time to get to know God on a personal level. When we take time to pray, we are speaking to God, and when we read God's Word, God is speaking to us.

Most of us want God's guidance for our lives, which I have found to be a day-by-day process that is introduced through reading and studying God's Word. It was over many years of being in God's Word that I began to understand with more clarity when it was God speaking to me. This is how you gain experience in knowing when it is God's voice speaking to your heart to help guide you in the right direction for your life; this happens over time, not overnight. I am still growing and learning more about God every day, and sometimes, I miss it. However, I would have not begun to know God at all if I had not first surrendered my life to Him through Jesus Christ.

There are no easy steps or process in learning God's voice and hearing direction for your life. You must surrender your life to Jesus Christ, deny yourself, and take up your cross and follow Jesus. In Luke 9:23, Jesus is speaking here, saying, *"If any man will come after me, let him deny himself, and take up his cross daily, and follow me."* When we take up our cross and follow Jesus, we are acknowledging the sacrifice that Jesus made on our behalf. It is only understandable that we would deny our desire to want to do life our own way. Anytime we deny ourselves to honor and bring glory to Jesus, this would be a good thing. Do not think that when you deny yourself to follow Jesus, you are giving up something grand and fabulous in your life. You are giving up nothing in comparison to what you will gain by receiving Jesus as your Lord and Savior. The scripture found in Romans 8:18 says it best, *"For I reckon that the sufferings of this present time are not worthy to be compared with the glory which shall be revealed in us."*

For whosoever will save his life shall lose it: but whosoever will lose his life for my sake, the same shall save it. (Luke 9:24)

Whatever we face in life, God has our answer, and when we have a relationship with Him, He will lead and guide us all the way to the end of our life's journey. In Psalm 48:14, *"For this God is our God for ever and ever: he will be our guide even unto death."* God is already in our tomorrows before we even get there. He is already aware of what we need and has prepared the way. That is why God and only God has our answers to any and every problem we face. God is omnipresent, so He is everywhere at the same time. He is omnipotent, so He has all power to take care of our every situation and circumstance. God is omniscient, which means He has divine foreknowledge of everything that exists, and the answers to every question, need, or want are found in the Word of God that you will find as you grow in your relationship with Him.

The devil wants us to believe that we are missing out on the better things in life and that we can make it on our own without God. But let me tell you, whether you are with God or without God, you will still have storms in life, but only having a life with God can give you the peace you need during those storms. I am a witness from experience that life is far better with God than without God. He has helped me through some difficult times. I am sure we all can say that life has been hard at times, and I know I have some witnesses out there who can agree—that God still can give you peace in the midst of any storm.

These things I have spoken unto you, that in me ye might have peace. In the world ye shall have tribulation: but be of good cheer; I have overcome the world. (John 16:33)

It is through those difficult days that we grow and see how God brings us through. Difficulties strengthen our faith and trust in God for the next time we face a hard time. It is like building blocks one upon another, going from one learned experience to the next. God is taking us from glory to glory as the Word of God says in 2 Corinthians 3:18, *"But we all, with open face beholding as in a glass the glory of the Lord, are changed into the same image from glory to glory, even as by the Spirit of the Lord."* God is shaping and molding us for the good and for His glory. However, I must inform you that this does not happen overnight. We change only as we surrender our life to the Lord. Otherwise, we will remain in the same stagnated way, never growing, never progressing, never changing, and never advancing to our next level in God.

God loves every effort that we make toward Him, and when we ask for His help, He will make certain that we receive the help we need. God will make sure that the right people come our way who can speak a word in due season that will encourage us at the right time. God will never leave us alone when we have asked for His help. Even though we don't find our names in the Bible regarding our personal situations, we will find help in God's Word that is relatable to what we are going through.

The Bible already tells us that there is nothing new under the sun as mentioned in Ecclesiastes 1:9. The saints of old went through things that are still common to us today, and their experiences are all written in the Word of God for us to learn from.

There hath no temptation taken you but such as is common to man: but God is faithful, who will not suffer you to be tempted above that ye are able; but will with the temptation also make a way to escape, that ye may be able to bear it. (1 Corinthians 10:13)

And there is no new thing under the sun. (Ecclesiastes 1:9)

We all want God to speak to us, especially in those urgent times that require immediate attention. Know that God is with you and speaking to you, but you must have an open and willing heart to hear Him through His Holy Spirit. The Holy Spirit will always bring the Word of God to your remembrance and reveal what is needed for every situation you face. However, if you are not reading God's Word, the Holy Spirit will have nothing to bring to your remembrance.

In John 14:26, *"But the Comforter, which is the Holy Ghost, whom the Father will send in my name, he shall teach you all things, and bring all things to your remembrance, whatsoever I have said unto you."* As you see here, for the Holy Spirit to bring anything to your remembrance (*memory*), it must already be in you. Read what you can even if it is a few verses a day, meditate on those verses, and pick back up where you left off for the next day. Don't allow the enemy to consume you with negative thoughts that you are not making any progress—that is a lie. You do what is comfortable for you, and don't be intimidated by what someone else is doing or what they are telling you. Be honest with yourself about what you can handle. The Holy Spirit works with all of us based on the level of where we are in our relationship with God. The more you pour into God by reading His Word, the more the Holy Spirit can pour back into you.

> *This book of the law shall not depart out of thy mouth; but thou shalt meditate therein day and night. (Joshua 1:8)*

CHAPTER 2

The Prophetic Message

A prophetic message should be a confirmation or an affirmation of what God has already spoken to you. God can speak to us through a prophetic message; however, the messengers do not always have to be preachers or ministers of the gospel but a person used by God at an appointed time. We should only want a *prophetic word* that confirms what we have already spoken to God about in prayer. If a *prophetic word, message, or word of encouragement* is needed for you, God will make sure He brings the right messenger your way. However, we are still to remain watchful because false prophets are out there who can lead you in a direction that is outside of God's plan for your life. As the scripture reminds us in 1 John 4:1, *"Beloved, believe not every spirit, but try the spirits whether they are of God: because many false prophets are gone out into the world."*

I remember hearing a minister say, "If the *prophetic word* spoken does not come to pass, then it was not prophetic." We must always test the spirits as the scripture says to see if what they are saying is aligned with the Word of God and agrees with what we are praying to God about.

In Matthew 24:24, *"For there shall arise false Christs, and false prophets, and shall shew great signs and wonders; insomuch that, if it were possible, they shall deceive the very elect."* Even the righteous (born-again believers) must stay alert—by praying, reading His Word, and remaining in close fellowship with God.

I hope you already know to stay away from fortune tellers, palm readers, and psychic networks. The Word of God places them under the same category as "false prophets" and "soothsayers." They are considered forms of "sorcery and witchcraft." They come by presenting a minor truth about yourself or a situation that is just enough to draw you in, but in the end, it will lead you to destruction. It is designed to pull you away from God and, ultimately, to destroy your soul. Anyone who says they have a special *prophetic word* from God for you, and that may be true, just remember 1 Peter 5:8, *"Be sober, be vigilant; because your adversary the devil, as a roaring lion, walketh about, seeking whom he may devour."*

I will share an example of how important it is to stay alert whenever a prophetic word is being spoken to you. Make sure of the authenticity of the words being spoken is true to what the Spirit of God has been speaking to you. When I was around twenty-six years old, a woman from the church I was attending wanted me to go with her to a church revival in a nearby city. She did not have a car and would need a ride, so I agreed to pick her up. Once we arrived at the church, it was already full of people, but the usher was able to find us a seat toward the back. The service was already in session, and the minister was randomly calling people to the altar where he was laying hands on them and prophesying.

From where we were sitting, I noticed that the minister kept looking my way. I said to myself, *I sure hope he does not call me up front.* And sure enough, he looked directly at me and said, "You right there."

I looked to my right, and I looked to my left; I even looked behind me, hoping he was speaking to someone else. But he wasn't. He said, "Yes, you, the one holding the baby in her arms."

I was holding the woman's baby who had invited me to the service. I passed her baby back to her, and I began walking up front to the altar. Reluctantly, I moved to the front and stood where they told me to stand, and he began prophesying over me.

I am not a person who looks for nor hopes for this sort of thing—to be called out in a congregation full of people. At this point, I was thinking, *I sure hope he does not lay his hands on me.* I am very particular about who lays hands on me when I am not familiar with the person's walk with God. I remember years ago, my mother telling me, "If ever somebody goes to lay hands on you, but you are unfamiliar with their walk with God, begin to pray in the Spirit [*tongues*] and pray the blood of Jesus over yourself and ask God to protect you." That was exactly what I began doing. I started to pray in the Spirit! Since I was praying in tongues, they did not know what I was saying because I was praying to God through His Holy Spirit to protect me.

For those of you who are not familiar with praying in the Spirit, I am referring to praying in an unknown language also known as *tongues.* This is where the Holy Spirit of God prays the perfect will of God through you to God on your behalf. I began praying in tongues softly under my breath to God for His protection over my life and to guard me against any unwelcoming spirits.

Just as the scripture says in 1 Corinthians 14:2, *"For he that speaketh in an unknown tongue speaketh not unto men, but unto God: for no man understandeth him; howbeit in the spirit he speaketh mysteries."* Thank God I knew I could go to God in prayer through His Holy Spirit, and I knew the perfect will of God was being prayed through me on my behalf. If you do not know what to do in a situation that could be potentially detrimental to your life and walk with God, you need to know the tools that are available to you through Jesus Christ. This is only for those who have received and made Jesus Christ the Lord of their life.

*(For the weapons of our warfare
are not carnal, but mighty through
God to the pulling down of strong
holds;) (2 Corinthians 10:4)*

As the minister began to prophesy over me, the other ministers on the floor surrounded me, and the head minister began to speak a so-called *prophetic message* to me. I say *so-called* only because it did not register with anything that I had been in prayer to God about or that I was believing God for. Remember what I just explained in the first paragraph that a *prophetic word and/or message* should confirm or affirm what God has already spoken to your heart. When a *prophetic word* comes to you, it should bring you peace and confirmation.

I cannot remember all of what this minister was saying to me because I was so busy praying in the Spirit and praying Jesus's blood over my life. All I know is that I could hear the people in the congregation, saying, "Oh, wow," and praising God as if what he was saying was so profound, and some of what I can remember him saying to me was amazing to hear; but as I mentioned before, I can only move forward on the fact that I was unaware of where he was coming from because this was not something that I was in prayer with God about.

If the *prophetic message* he spoke to me that day does not come to pass, then it was not a *prophetic message* that was meant for me. If it does come to pass, then it was a *prophetic message* for me. It has now been over thirty years ago, and I'm not saying that it still cannot happen because it could. There have been several examples in the Bible of prophecies that came to pass many years later after they were spoken.

I encourage you to read the beautiful prophecy in Zechariah chapter 14, where he has prophesied the return of Jesus Christ that every believer is still watching and waiting with great anticipation for its fulfillment. We should know by now that God does not operate on our timetable. God can bring things to pass at any time in our life, but it must be in His time and according to His plan and purpose.

There was another minister who spoke a *prophetic message* to me that happened later in my thirties, and this prophecy immediately registered and ministered to my spirit. There was an instant connection right away with what this minister of God was speaking to me; it confirmed and affirmed what I had already prayed to God about. That *prophetic message* brought forth comfort to my soul and spirit with an assurance that God had heard my prayers. Not long after this *prophetic message* was spoken to me, it was manifested in my life. Therefore, the words spoken to me through this messenger were true *prophetic words/messages and/or words of encouragement* that brought edification, exhortation, and comfort to me at that time, and the prophecy given to me that day did happen.

> *But he that prophesieth speaketh unto men to edification, and exhortation, and comfort. (1 Corinthians 14:3)*

CHAPTER 3

Knowing God's Voice

When we think about the saints in the Bible, they talked to God regularly, and it was evident that they had a personal and close relationship with Him. When an angel of God relayed a message to them, they were willing to do whatever He asked because they had already built an established trust in who God is. For example, God called Abraham His friend, and when God spoke, Abraham would listen and respond in obedience to whatever God would ask him to do. We discussed earlier how prayer is having a conversation with God, and when we pray, we speak to God, and through God's Word, He speaks to us. Therefore, learning God's voice first begins with having a relationship that will grow and develop as you spend time getting to know Him through His Word.

> *Abraham believed God, and it was imputed unto him for righteousness: and he was called the Friend of God. (James 2:23)*

When the angel of the Lord came to Mary, she was told that the Holy Ghost would come upon her and overshadow her and that she would conceive and bring forth a son and call His name Jesus. How did she reply to that? We see her response in Luke 1:38, *"Behold the handmaid of the Lord; be it unto me according to thy word."* This response came from true love and a committed relationship with God. She was already a witness to the goodness of God from her time spent and life experience with God. Mary knew she could trust whatever He presented to her because she understood that it would ultimately work out for her good. Although at times we may find it hard to do what God is speaking to our hearts, but as we grow in our relationship with Him, we know that He has our best interest at heart and will bring us through.

The saints mentioned thus far, we see they were able to know God's voice based on their time spent with God. There is no quick fix to this; you cannot suddenly know and hear the voice of God if you have made no attempt to get to know Him first. You cannot expect to get saved today and automatically know and understand God's voice tomorrow. You will become more familiar with His voice as you spend time with Him—by reading His Word and by experiencing tests and trials through your life's journey with God.

How quickly we come to know and learn God's voice is up to us; it is based on how much time we spend getting to know Him. This would be the same as any other relationship we have. There are some relationships where we may feel like we have known that person for a long time, and as we are getting to know them, it seems so easy. We love going out with them and talking to them on the phone, so we set time aside just for them. However, with some people, it may be hard at first, and the conversation may not flow as easily; but over time, we find they turn out to be one of our better relationships. Why is that? It is because we took time to learn and know that person's heart. As a result, the relationship can develop into something meaningful and worthwhile.

Our relationship with God is more meaningful and by far more important than any other relationship we will ever have in life. We need to make it our priority to develop an intimate relationship with God so we can hear when He is speaking to us. There is no other way we can expect to recognize the difference between God and other voices if we do not learn through His Word how He speaks and what He feels. As the scripture says in Hebrews 4:15, *"For we have not an high priest which cannot be touched with the feeling of our infirmities."* God has feelings that we need to tap into to understand how much He loves us and wants to have an intimate relationship with us. However, we can miss all of what He wants us to know if we are unwilling to share our hearts with Him as He wants to share His heart with us.

When we think about our close relationships, we can see how we have come to know their likes, dislikes, and characteristics. We know and recognize the voices of our spouse, family, and friends, but sometimes, we still struggle in knowing the voice of God. This is why I say that it all comes back to how much time we spend getting to know Him.

For example, nobody can fool me into thinking that they are my husband because I know his voice, ways, and mannerisms. It is the same way with God. I have come to learn and know God's voice over the years and throughout my walk with Him. I have learned what God loves and what God hates, and every day I spend with God, I continue to learn more about who He is.

We can learn a lot about God just by reading here in Proverbs about the six things that God hates and are an abomination to Him. In Proverbs 6:17–19, *"A proud look, a lying tongue, and hands that shed innocent blood, An heart that deviseth wicked imaginations, feet that be swift in running to mischief, A false witness that speaketh lies, and he that soweth discord among brethren."* We do not search to learn and understand the scriptures (*God's Word*) as if we are trying to obtain some goal of achievement but, rather, as something we want to do so we can have a better relationship with Him.

Learning the likes and dislikes of a person in your relationship is one way toward understanding and knowing what makes up the character of who they are. Taking time out of our day to read, study, or just sit quietly in prayer is not for God; it is for us. God knows who He is, and we are the ones needing to know Him better. When you know someone's character, you are better equipped to recognize when they are presented to you. This is why spending time with God is so important so we can learn and be familiar with the different characteristics between God and Satan.

The devil is a liar and an accuser of the brethren, and he consumes all evil that exists in the world as we know it. God is love, sovereign, forgiving, longsuffering, merciful, all-powerful, and just. One of the easiest ways to know when it is God speaking to you is to follow the love factor. God's focus will always be founded on love and for our ultimate good.

When you stay in prayer and in God's Word, you will come to know that not every voice, sign, dream, or signal is from God, and not every unexpected or unimaginable voice or sign is from the devil. Therefore, you will not be able to recognize the difference if you are not spending time with God.

God Speaks to the Backslider

God loves the righteous and is always calling His own to return to Him. If you are currently in a backslidden position, please know that God is waiting for you to repent so He can receive you with open arms. For this to happen, you must have a willing heart to change and to turn away from the sin you are in. Do not listen to the lies of the enemy (Satan) and allow your walk with God to end there. God is about restoration and has made provisions for us whenever we do things that are displeasing and not within the will of God for our life.

In Jeremiah 3:22, God is saying to all who have gone outside of His will to *"Return, ye backsliding children, and I will heal your backslidings."* God is always wanting to restore His people. God will never leave His children stranded even when we have sinned and gone astray. The Bible says in Luke 15:10, *"Likewise, I say unto you, there is joy in the presence of the angels of God over one sinner that repenteth."* There will be rejoicing in heaven when you repent and return to God.

Please know that if you have backslidden, this does not mean you are no longer saved, but it does mean you have become out of fellowship with God and must repent. As long as you have breath in your body, you can come back to God. However, I would advise anyone whether a backslider or a nonbeliever to not linger in sin or become comfortable with a sinful lifestyle. Do not take for granted the mercies and grace of God or think it does not matter because you have time to get your life together. It does matter, and it matters a great deal; unfortunately, some may not come to realize the true depth of their consequences until it is too late for them to make a change.

In Psalm 37:9–10, *"For evildoers shall be cut off: For yet a little while, and the wicked shall not be: yea, thou shalt diligently consider his place, and it shall not be."* In Proverbs 6:15, *"Therefore shall his calamity come suddenly; suddenly shall he be broken without remedy."* When you are doing your own thing, you tend not to care about the consequences that come down the road, but I will tell you that the end to all sin is death. You do not want to remember at the end of your life the opportunities you dismissed to get your life right with God. The Bible tells us that the time will come when no man can stand unless they are covered by the blood of Jesus. It is only by the blood of Jesus that we are forgiven and restored.

> *For the great day of his wrath is come; and who shall be able to stand? (Revelations 6:17)*

> *In whom we have redemption through his blood, the forgiveness of sins, according to the riches of his grace. (Ephesians 1:7)*

Generally, when believers sin, it creates a turbulence inside that does not allow us to rest in that sin. Just knowing that we have hurt the heart of God makes us want to get back in right standing with Him. This is what having a relationship will do: When you hurt the one you love, you want to make things right between you and the other person. A nonbeliever has no problem indulging in their sin, nor do they have any remorse or desire to repent.

Romans 1:28 reads, *"God gave them over to a reprobate mind, to do those things which are not convenient."* Those of a reprobate mind as stated here are not the same as those who have backslidden in their relationship with God. The dictionary's definition of *reprobate* is a person rejected by God and is beyond hope of salvation. These persons have no desire or heart to follow God.

The dictionary's definition of a *backslider* means to relapse into bad habits, sinful behavior, or undesirable activities. A backslider may have given their life to Jesus but has fallen away for a season. These persons can repent and turn back to God to regain right fellowship with Him. Only those who already have a relationship with God can do this. A person with a reprobate mind has no prior relationship with God, nor do they desire to have one. Only you and God know whether you have a heart that wants to change or a heart of disregard toward the things of God.

However, if you are worried about hurting the heart of God, and you know what you are doing goes against His Word, but you desire to get your life in order, God knows this as well. God knows when we want to do the right thing but are having difficulty doing so and need His help to not do the things we ought not. All we need to do is ask God for help, and He will make sure we have the help we need.

> *God is our refuge and strength, a very present help in trouble. (Psalm 46:1)*

It used to be hard to understand why people would come to the altar for rededication after backsliding. Jesus Christ made access available for us to come to God on our own by what He did for us on the cross. However, if you do not have the knowledge and understanding of this benefit, then by all means, please go to the altar for prayer. I do understand there are other reasons why some may still want to come forward. Sometimes, it may be just for support or to rejoin or rededicate themselves back to the church. Of course, if you need someone to help you with praying, then please go to the altar for further assistance. I just want to make sure everyone knows that you can always go to God directly on your own.

Once you have given your life to the Lord, you do not have to wait to go up front to rededicate your life back to Him when you have gone astray. It would be like you are asking God to save you for the second time. We should know from God's Word where He has stated that we are sealed and that no one can pluck us out of His hand. The following scripture from Ephesians 4:30 says, *"And grieve not the holy Spirit of God, whereby ye are sealed unto the day of redemption."* Also, here in John 10:29, Jesus is saying, *"My Father, which gave them me, is greater than all; and no man is able to pluck them out of my Father's hand."* All you would need to do is repent and ask God for forgiveness, and He will forgive you and restore you back to right fellowship with Him.

You must get to know God for yourself so you are not always relying on someone else's relationship to help pull you through. I want you to know what is already available to you. Why go to others for something that you already have access to do on your own? As I mentioned before, I know we all can benefit from the prayers of others, and we most definitely should. However, let us keep in mind the times when the church doors are not open, or your close friends and family may not be available. We must know what to do and how to go to God for ourselves if it is late in the midnight hour. Develop a relationship with

God now so you are comfortable in knowing how to call on Him for yourself. Nobody can wish this for you; you must have the desire for a personal and intimate relationship with God on your own. God wants all of us to know that we can call on Him any time of any day, and He is there as the scripture says here, *"Draw nigh to God, and he will draw nigh to you"* (James 4:8).

CHAPTER 5

You Are Forgiven

God says you are forgiven as you forgive others. But what about when you have a hard time forgiving yourself? A lot of us still have a problem letting go of our past mistakes even though we know we can't take them back or change the course of their consequences. Thankfully, God is faithful and just to forgive us and to cleanse us from all unrighteousness. As stated in 1 John 1:9, *"If we confess our sins, he is faithful and just to forgive us our sins, and to cleanse us from all unrighteousness."* This is wonderful news, but while God has forgiven us of our sins, we must rid the thoughts of our past mistakes. Our past mistakes can create a stronghold and make us question where we stand in our relationship with God.

Having any kind of heaviness or distance in our relationship with God will no doubt affect our ability in wanting to spend time with God and, therefore, affect our ability to hear from God. This has always been the enemy's goal—to bring condemnation from our past mistakes hoping to shake our confidence in knowing who we are in Christ. We all have struggled at some point with being reminded of our past sins. This is one of the hardest battles we face as born-again believers, but God has provided us with His Holy Spirit to help us deal with the thoughts and struggles of the mind. We can ask the Holy Spirit to give us the power to overcome temptation.

Never think that you are too far gone to receive any help from God. This is a lie from the devil that he wants you to believe. The devil loves for you to stay in sin and remain out of fellowship with God. Do not listen to the devil's voice through the wrong influences that he sends from bad associations and from your own negative thoughts. My suggestion is to always listen to the positive influences that lead you back to God. What will help you is to surround yourself with godly and positive associations and activities that can help you grow in your relationship with God. We must practice discipline by daily dying to the fleshly desires that work to pull us away from God, and we all know what can pull us away.

Nobody can do this for you; you have to want to do the right thing that pleases God for yourself. There is no sin, issue, or problem that you have that is too much or too strong that the power of God cannot handle or remove from your life. We sometimes make things hard on ourselves when we do not follow simple practices to help move us forward in victory. We spend a lot of time playing back past mistakes and wishing we had made better decisions; however, this does not bring about any changeable results. The best thing for us to do for a better outcome is to be prepared and think about what could be the end consequential result. If it is regret, then don't do it.

When God tells us to remember not the former things, this is not only for what we have done but also for what others have done to us. If God can blot out our transgressions, we surely can work to do the same with other people who have hurt or wronged us in some way. We have the capability to free ourselves from so much heartache and pain by just releasing others from the negative tape that replays in our minds. A great scripture to meditate on is found in Isaiah 43:18–19, *"Remember ye not the former things, neither consider the things of old. Behold, I will do a new thing, now it shall spring forth; shall ye not know it? I will even make a way in the wilderness, and rivers in the desert."*

God, through His precious Holy Spirit, is forever changing us into the image of Jesus Christ for our good and for His glory. However, none of this happens unless we are willing to change and welcome (invite) the Holy Spirit in to begin that good work in us. I know for myself there is always something God is working with me on, whether it is an attitude adjustment, selfishness, bitterness, or whatever it may be; the list can go on and on. Please know, for as long as we are in this earthly body (the flesh), there will always be room for change and improvement. This is a good thing; we should not want God to stop working on us and changing us for the better. The change is the evidence (proof) that shows we are moving forward in our relationship with God. I would even say that if you cannot see where you have changed over the years, hopefully for the good, then I would be concerned. Remember, you must be willing and open before any change can take place. God will never override your will (decision).

> *Being confident of this very thing, that he which hath begun a good work in you will perform it until the day of Jesus Christ: (Philippians 1:6)*

CHAPTER 6

Be Constant in Prayer

Being constant in prayer is having open communication with God that never ends. This means our lines of communication with God should always remain open. I know you are wondering how can this be done and still be able to talk to other people. It is easy, and those of you who are already born-again believers may notice that you do this as well. I know for myself I always make it clear to God that He is welcomed into every area of my life. When I pray, I ask God to order my steps and direct my paths daily. In doing this, I place my trust in knowing that God is directing me throughout the day. It helps me to trust my inner core decisions because I have given Him access to my life. If I make a decision that is not the best, God will still work it out for my good because I am trusting in Him. The scripture that helps me have peace when things seem to be in disarray is Romans 8:28, *"And we know that all things work together for good to them that love God, to them who are the called according to his purpose."* I know that I love God, and I know I am called for His purpose, so when things get hard, I know it will come together for my good.

When you have a relationship with God, you are connected to Him in such a way that you know He is available to listen to you, and you are available to listen to Him. We are not to call on Him as if He were a genie. He is God Almighty, who will never leave you nor forsake you. He is to be honored, adored, and always worshipped. When we have an attitude of gratitude and a heart of thanksgiving, we then are acknowledging God the Awesome "I AM!"

The Bible says that whoever comes to God must first acknowledge that He is who He says He is and that He is a rewarder for those who diligently seek Him. As mentioned here in Hebrews 11:6, *"But without faith it is impossible to please him: for he that cometh to God must believe that he is, and that he is a rewarder of them that diligently seek him."*

It would be hard to have a prayer life if you do not know or do not acknowledge that who you are coming to is more than able to meet and understand your needs; otherwise, why come? You may feel that you are not worthy to approach the creator of all heaven and earth, and you are correct; you are not and neither am I or anyone else. However, because of the goodness of God, He sent His Son Jesus Christ to die for our sins, and God raised Jesus from the dead; therefore, He now sits on the right hand of God the Father and has made available to us all spiritual blessings.

We now have the right to come boldly to the throne of grace and ask what we want according to His will. God welcomes us to come and sit and have a conversation with Him through prayer. Remember, you can only approach Him through and by His Son Jesus Christ. Jesus Christ has made it possible for all of us to come to God, as we see here in the following scriptures: in Hebrews 4:16, *"Let us therefore come boldly unto the throne of grace, that we may obtain mercy, and find grace to help in time of need,"* and in Ephesians 1:3, *"Blessed be the God and Father of our Lord Jesus Christ, who hath blessed us with all spiritual blessings in heavenly places in Christ."*

During hard times, we generally think to go to God first, but what about when times are good? He still should be the first one we go to and give thanks for His goodness. He is not only God when you are going through the darkness of the valleys, but He is God when you are on top of the highest mountain. We should seek God and praise God in the good as well as the bad times. Let us stay mindful of this scripture in Hebrews 13:15, *"By him therefore let us offer the sacrifice of praise to God continually, that is, the fruit of our lips giving thanks to his name."*

Since the Word of God is the primary way that God speaks to us, then it is even more powerful that when we pray, we pray by using God's Word. This will help us to have more confidence in knowing that we are praying for the will of God. All our prayers are welcomed by God, and feel free to ask and seek God on anything you would like but just know that if it is not in His will, you will not get the answer you want.

We know that healing is in the Word of God, and we know praying to be delivered from bad behavior is the will of God, but praying to get somebody else's husband or wife or for God to hurt someone because they did you wrong is not in the will of God. God tells us to pray for our enemies and to pray for those who despitefully use us. God tells us to bless and curse not. God says, "Vengeance is mine, I will repay."

God will take care of any and every situation if something has been wrongfully done against us. God wants us to keep our hearts right and pray, forgive, and bless them. John 15:7 says, *"If ye abide in me, and my words abide in you, ye shall ask what ye will, and it shall be done unto you."* The keyword is *abiding;* Jesus is speaking here and saying that if we abide in Him and His Words abide in us, then we can ask what we will, and it will be done for us. When you spend time with God and acknowledge and recognize the holiness that resides within Him, you will not be asking for anything that you know dishonors or displeases the creator of heaven and earth. You will realize at that moment before you even attempt to pray that you are off course. The Holy Spirit of God will make sure you know in your heart that you need to rethink what you are asking God for. Either way, even if you try to slip it through and it is not the will of God, you can rest assured it will not happen.

How many of you think that when you pray, you must be in a certain position or posture, or do you believe that if you are not on your knees or have your eyes closed, you are not really praying for God to hear you? Well, let me free you up in this area because that is absolutely not true. I know, on multiple occasions, I have had my mouth closed and was praying to God, and guess what? I know He heard me and still answered me. How do I know this? It's because my spirit was connected to His Spirit, and my heart and attitude were toward God. Read here in Isaiah 65:24, *"And it shall come to pass, that before they call, I will answer; and while they are yet speaking, I will hear."* That is how I know because the Word of God says so. You must believe Him at His Word and have faith in knowing that what you have read is the truth!

You do not have to bow your head or close your eyes or move your lips to be praying to God. Prayer is communication within your spirit that connects to God's Spirit. Prayer should not be a formality but an attitude of the heart. You can bow your head, close your eyes, and even move your lips, and still, your heart could be far from God. Just like it says in Matthew 15:8, *"This people draweth nigh unto me with their mouth, and honoureth me with their lips; but their heart is far from me."* Remember, it is not the posture of your prayers that matter; it is the condition of your heart toward God and whether you have faith and trust in what God has said in His Word.

I do not pray with my mouth closed regularly, but what I am wanting you to know is that you can be in any position and posture to pray to God. There are times I believe when it is best for me to be quiet and be in an attitude of prayer where my heart is in tune with God. Then I have no problem doing just that because I know God still hears me when I call on Him. This brings me back to our earlier discussion on relationships.

I would never disrespect my relationship with God by not honoring Him in my approach to prayer. Therefore, I am free to pray to God whichever way I choose to, as long as my prayers are with a sincere heart, giving reverence to who He is, and having faith and trust in knowing God is more than able to do what I am praying to Him for.

> *The LORD is nigh unto all them that call upon him, to all that call upon him in truth. (Psalm 145:18)*

And all things, whatsoever ye shall ask in prayer, believing, ye shall receive. (Matthew 21:22)

And all things, whatsoever ye shall ask in prayer, believing, ye shall receive. (Matthew 21:22)

CHAPTER 7

Honoring God: The Awesome I AM!

Everything that has been discussed in this book about knowing and recognizing when it is God speaking to you, you cannot begin to start this conversation without first honoring God and realizing the awesomeness of who you are speaking to and who is speaking back to you. When we approach God on any level, we must first recognize that He is the "I AM." We honor God whenever we give respect, reverence, and recognition to the greatness of who He is.

In Psalm 33:8, *"Let all the earth fear the Lord: let all the inhabitants of the world stand in awe of him."* We must first notice the greatness and recognize the privilege that has been given to us through Jesus Christ that allows us to be invited to sit in His presence.

If we fail to reverence and recognize all that He has done and continues to do for us, we lessen our ability to hear from God. How can we expect to hear from God if we have no honor or respect for who He says He is? God says in His Word that He only speaks His secrets to those who reverence Him; this is mentioned in Psalm 25:14, *"The secret of the LORD is with them that fear him; and he will shew them his covenant."* We are the same way; we only share our close and intimate thoughts with those who have shown an interest in knowing who we are and who we know cares about us as well. It says in Proverbs 8:17, *"I love them that love me; and those that seek me early shall find me."*

God knows what is in our hearts and the motives behind what we do. He knows if we are sincere when we come to Him or if we are just going through the motions. God knows He is still working with us, and He knows how long it will take to get us where He wants us to be. Please do not be intimidated or feel there is no use in coming to God because you don't have a good relationship with Him. I have been saved for almost fifty years, and I am still growing and will continue to grow in my relationship with God. We all will be growing until we go home to be with the Lord. The key is still growing; we must keep moving forward in our growth process with our relationship with God. No matter how long we have been saved, none of us will ever arrive to the point where we can say, *"I know all there is about God,"* not if you are still living on this earth. True, we have learned a lot along our journey, but there will always be more we can learn, and there will always be more room for us to grow.

I can remember the times when my sisters and I would be sitting around the kitchen table or in my parents' bedroom talking with my mother about the Lord and His goodness. We all should be able to speak about the goodness of God and reflect on how He has made a difference in our life. Everyone should have a story to tell, some good and some bad, but still able to say, "Thanks be to God for all He has done."

The Bible always mentions the importance of giving God the praise that is due to His Name and for us to have a heart of thankfulness. When we come to God in prayer, we should start by entering His presence with praise and thanksgiving before ever listing our wants and desires. Just think about how you would feel if you were in a relationship, and they were always coming to you with requests and demands; it would make you wonder if they were in the relationship only for what they could get out of it and not because they love or care about you.

> *Enter into his gates with thanksgiving, and into his courts with praise: be thankful unto him, and bless his name. (Psalm 100:4)*

The Bible teaches us to share the goodness of God with our children and to speak of it when we lie down and when we rise—which means at all times. The scripture in Deuteronomy 6:7 is excellent to this point: *"And thou shalt teach them diligently unto thy children, and shalt talk of them when thou sittest in thine house, and when thou walkest by the way, and when thou liest down, and when thou risest up."* Speak about God's goodness throughout your journey. If you do not speak it out loud, you can speak it with your lifestyle. How we live our life at times can speak louder than our mouths ever could. Doing the right thing and being a person of integrity can be a powerful witness to other people. Either way, be a positive example for the good of God's kingdom, so when we have passed on, we have left behind a mark that represents Jesus and glorifies God.

> *But none of these things move me, neither count I my life dear unto myself, so that I might finish my course with joy, and the ministry, which I have received of the Lord Jesus, to testify the gospel of the grace of God. (Acts 20:24)*

It is all about God and giving Him the glory that is due to His Name. God is the creator of all things, and we must realize that no man lives to himself and dies to himself. We were created for God's glory, yet He still gives us the freedom and choice to choose and serve Him. God did not want robots, nor did He make us be at His beckoned call. However, God desires to have a relationship with us where we freely come to Him on our own with loving service and sincere worship.

Jesus brought freedom and liberty when He came to save the world. He became a ransom for many who were living in their sins and were headed for destruction with a fate that was damn to burn in hell. Please be reminded of this following scripture anytime you think that you are living solely for your own purposes; it is found in 2 Corinthians 5:21, *"For he hath made him to be sin for us, who knew no sin; that we might be made the righteousness of God in him."* Jesus did all of this for us. He came down from His glory in heaven so that we might have life and have it more abundantly and gave us hope for eternal life.

The story of Noah in the book of Genesis talks about how God found no one righteous within the earth, so He destroyed it with a flood and started all over again. When God sent Jesus, His only Son, it was a beautiful touch of His grace and mercy on all the generations that came after the flood. We can see all around us how evil the world has become, and only because of what Jesus did for us on the cross makes it possible for us to receive Him as our Lord and Savior. It is only by God's mercies that we are not consumed but given a chance to not be damned to a hell that we are deserving of.

When God looks at born-again believers, He sees the blood of redemption and the righteousness of His Son Jesus. The next time you see the rainbow in the sky, this is the promise God made to the world that He would never again destroy the earth by a flood. The story of the rainbow is found in Genesis 9:12–13, *"And God said, This is the token of the covenant which I make between me and you and every living creature that is with you, for perpetual generations: I do set my bow in the cloud, and it shall be for a token of a covenant between me and the earth."*

> *And I will establish my covenant with you; neither shall all flesh be cut off any more by the waters of a flood; neither shall there any more be a flood to destroy the earth.*
> *(Genesis 9:11)*

Whenever we acknowledge the Awesome I AM and place our trust and faith in God, we can be assured that He will always take our relationship with Him to another level. Just as I mentioned earlier, the scripture found in 2 Corinthians 3:18, *"But we all, with open face beholding as in a glass the glory of the Lord, are changed into the same image from glory to glory, even as by the Spirit of the Lord."* This means we are being changed and transformed daily into who God wants us to be. This is great news because we are not expected to change overnight; it is a process. As we learn more about God through reading His Word, we will continue to build a closer relationship with Him, and by this, we will come to know when it is God's voice speaking to us.

> *He that is of God heareth God's words: ye therefore hear them not, because ye are not of God. (John 8:47)*

> *My sheep hear my voice, and I know them, and they follow me. (John 10:27)*

*To hear and know God's voice, we
must first have a relationship with God
through and by His Son Jesus Christ.*

*Jesus saith unto him, I am the way, the
truth, and the life: no man cometh unto
the Father, but by me. (John 14:6)
For there is one God, and one mediator between God
and men, the man Christ Jesus; (1 Timothy 2:5)*

*As we surrender our life to Jesus Christ,
and begin to make it our business
to spend time getting to know God
through His Word, then God will speak
to us and we will know it is Him!*

For those who desire God's gift of salvation, say this prayer with a sincere and ready heart to receive!

Dear Lord Jesus, I believe in my heart and confess with my mouth that you are the Son of the living God! Please forgive me for all my past, present, and future sins. I ask for you to come into my heart and save me and change me into the person you would have me to be. Thank you for all you did for me by shedding your blood and dying on the cross. I believe God raised you from the dead, and I receive you as my Lord and Savior. In Jesus name, Amen!

For those who confessed that prayer with a sincere heart, congratulations and welcome to the family of God! God's Holy Spirit will teach, lead, comfort, and guide you as He begins to transform you into His likeness. As you continue in your walk with God, you will begin to see yourself changing for the good. Most importantly, you are now born-again and saved for all eternity! Please find yourself a Bible-teaching church so you can begin to learn and grow in the Word of God.

ABOUT THE AUTHOR

Jacqui D. Williams-Skipwith is the author of four books: *How Do I Know I Am Really Saved?*, *The Importance of Tithes and Offerings, God Is Speaking to You, and Life after Death: Heaven and Hell Are Real Places*. Her primary mission and objective in writing quick reference handbooks is to give the reader a brief glimpse into the knowledge and understanding of God's Word and to increase their desire for a better relationship with Him. Through her writings, she shares her life experiences from the topics given to her by the direction of the Holy Spirit of God.

You may purchase the author's books on:

Amazon, Barnes and Noble, Apple iTunes, and various other platforms

View the author's pages on:

www.amazon.com/author/jacquidwilliams

www.goodreads.com

Your feedback is welcomed!